USBORNE

SPACE PUZZLES

Illustrated by The Boy Fitz Hammond, Ana Bermejo, Samara Hardy, Helen Prole, Daniela Dogliani, Sean Sims and Gareth Williams

Designed by Sharon Cooper

Written by Kate Nolan

It's dinner time on the space station. Can each astronaut have one of every item on the menu? 1

Can you fill in the missing vowels to complete these planet names?

2

V_N_S	M_RC_RY	N_PT_N_	J_P_T_R
S_T_RN	M_RS	_ _ RTH	_R_N_S

Can you circle these 5 parts of the picture?

3

Which radio telescope is receiving the alien's message?

Find and circle...

...2 packets of seeds...

...an alien...

...2 snails...

...and a watering can.

Can you find a nine-letter word in the square below? Move from one letter to the next along the dotted lines, using each letter only once.

7

The space explorers are going to the mysterious Square Galaxy. How many squares do the stars make altogether?

8

In the grid below, the numbers in every 3-square row, column and diagonal add up to 15. Write the missing numbers on the empty planets.

9

Spot 5 differences between the pictures below.

Can you fit the aliens' names into the grid?

GLURNAK

ERKNOODLE

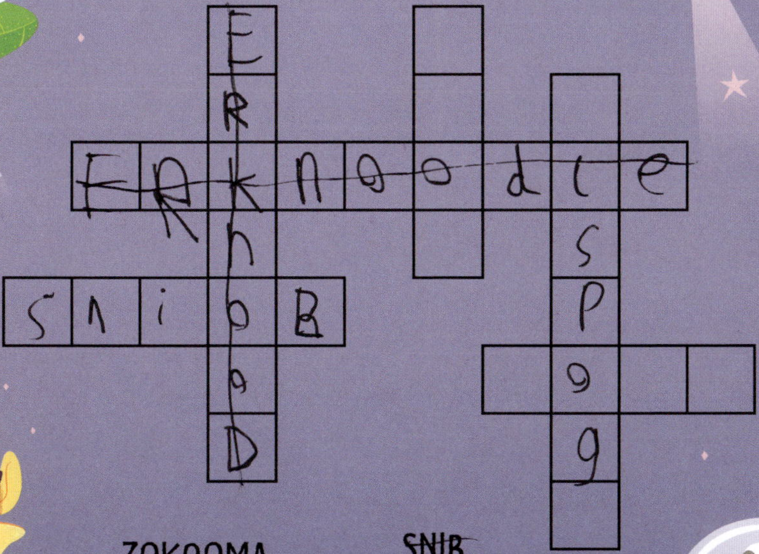

ZOKOOMA

SNIB

PODOX

SPOG

Draw the other half of this rocket, using the grid to help you.

Fill in the grid so that all four symbols appear in every row and column.

Which of the photos at the bottom has just been taken?

Follow the trails to find out which astronaut will carry their flag to Captain Camilla.

Can you draw a line to connect each pair of matching shapes? The lines can go up, across or down, but not diagonally. Only one line is allowed in each square, and they can't cross each other.

>> Example >>

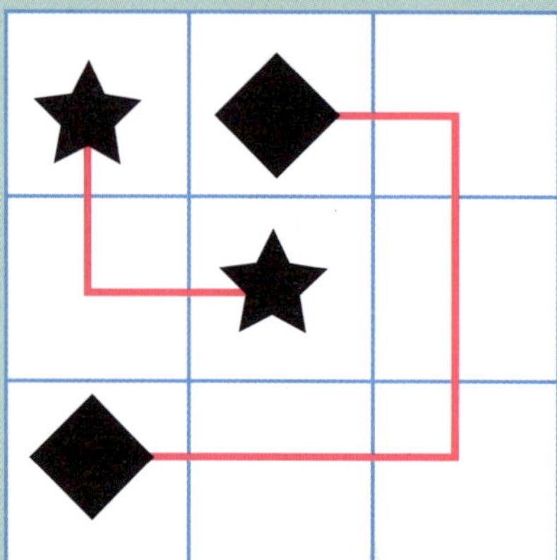

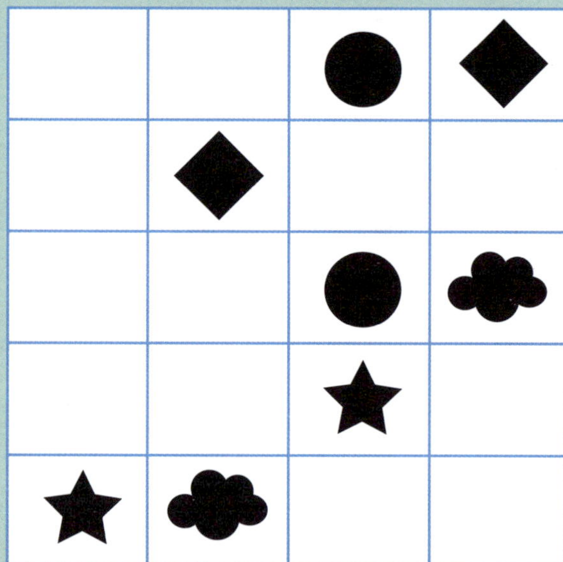

Spot 5 differences between the pictures below.

Can you fill in the missing vowels to complete these space travel words?

R_CK_T _XPL_R_

_RB_T L_ _NCH

PL_N_T M_SS_ _N

G_L_XY SH_TTL_

Can you help the robots find these three groups of cells in the grid below?

Leda has planned a route back to her home planet. It takes exactly 30 hours. The numbers in the circles show the time for each section. Can you find the correct route?

Can you fit these types of spacecraft into the grid?

TELESCOPE
SHUTTLE
CAPSULE
ORBITER
LANDER
PROBE

In the space race, Urk finished behind Zooble but ahead of Splog. Frimp didn't come first, but beat Urk. The name of the alien who came last begins with 'Z'. Write the aliens' names on the scoreboard below.

SCOREBOARD

1st..............................

2nd................. 3rd.................

4th................. 5th.................

Can you find these space words in the grid below?

		T	A	S	F	L	V		
	S	E	S	C	B	A	I	C	
N	L	M	T	L	L	R	O	L	M
E	T	O	E	G	A	L	A	X	Y
B	E	C	R	R	C	M	K	T	E
U	N	U	O	O	K	T	O	J	S
L	A	Y	I	E	H	I	S	O	C
A	L	F	D	T	O	B	U	P	N
	P	T	N	E	L	R	B	T	
		R	T	M	E	O	T		

ASTEROID
METEOR
COMET
MOON
STAR

ORBIT
PLANET
NEBULA
GALAXY
BLACK HOLE

This space station takes 90 minutes to orbit the Earth. Look at the screens and work out how many times each astronaut has gone around the Earth in the time they've been training.

Can you circle these 5 parts of the picture?

Write a word on each screen that can be made by changing just one letter of the word before it. There is a clue for each word to help you.

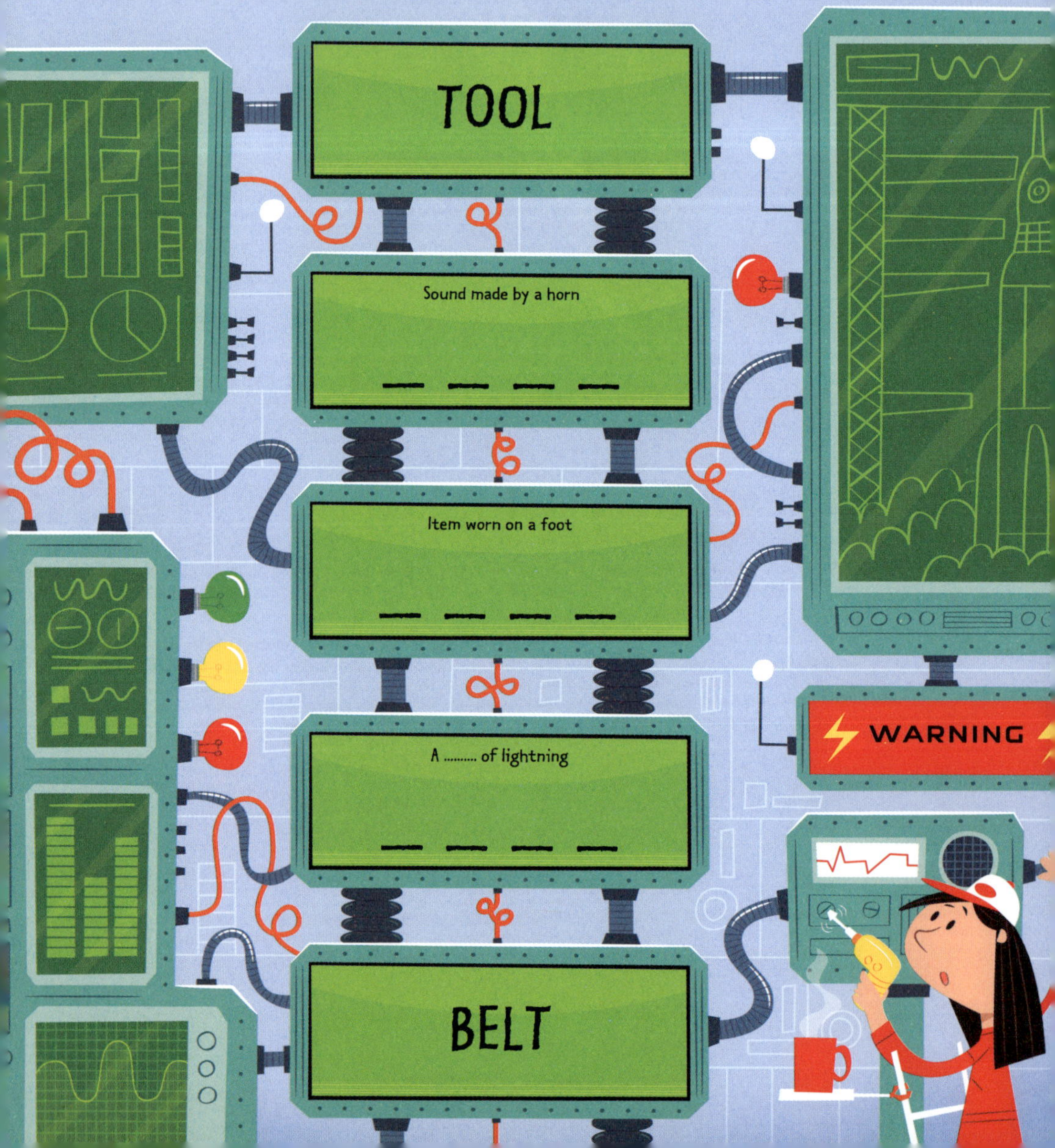

Which square at the bottom is not part of the picture?

Which of the nanobots at the bottom can find a way through the wires to defeat the computer virus?

Use the code below to read the alien's message.

Spot 5 differences between the pictures below.

30

Can you fit the words below into the grid?

MISSION CONTROL

DATA

MAPS

SCREENS

COMPUTERS

Each pilot only collects space rocks with a number that can be divided by the number on their spaceship. Circle the one who will collect the most rocks.

32

The space explorers need to charge their ship, but they only have 45 credits left. Each power cell on the charge bar costs 5 credits to fill. Shade in the cells to see if they have enough to reach the green zone on the bar.

Are there more aliens with three eyes or four eyes?

Answer: ....

Can you fill in the blank moon rocks, so that each number is the sum of the two directly beneath it?

Can you help the crew find a route through the galaxy? First, cross out these squares:
H2, C1, F4, B1, A3, C4, G4, C2, F2, A4, E2, C3, E4, G2, A5, D4.

Now trace the route through the squares with no Xs to lead them to their destination.

Find and circle 3 green moon rocks, 2 flags, 4 golf balls and a shovel.

Can you fit the astronauts' names into the grid?

38

Use the clues to find out which food each astronaut will choose, and draw a line to match them up.

Zoe needs to type in a number to start up the rover. Can you find it on the rocks below? It can be divided by 2, 3, 4, 6 and 8.

Can you circle these 5 parts of the picture?

40

Follow the trails to find out which alien is flying to planet Flurgal.

Bella and Bill are blasting asteroids to clear the way for their spaceship. For every 1 that Bella blasts, Bill gets 2. Write how many each person gets next to their name.

Bella: ....

Bill: ....

Fill in the grid so all the letters in the word STAR appear in every row and column.

R			
S	T	A	
		T	
	S		

Find these two groups of spaceships in the picture below.

Follow the lines to find out which astronaut is going to enter the Space Pod on planet Ploot.

This grid is made up of 6 blocks, each with 6 squares. Fill in the blank squares so that each block, row and column contains all the numbers 1 to 6.

4		3		1	
	1				
				3	2
3	4				
				4	
	3		5		6

Can you find the aliens' names in the grid?

L N B T S C Y D Q R
L E Z K R O L K I K
S O N M I N P X E Y
I I O O L A L D H G
N B L P N P U L R A
U I E N O W R O L T
R T Y R I N Z G S A
J O V E X M A F V R
Y H T I Z E L D U K
J R F R O Z O T H U

ZELDUK
LOOPONA
PLURZAL
KROLKIK
JOVEX
FROZOT
OOLA
ZORG
REBI
NURJ

48

Cross out every letter that is one of a pair. Then unscramble the remaining letters to find out which planet Annabel is exploring.

Solve the calculations to find out these spaceships' performance scores. Then add up each one's answers and circle the best spaceship.

Acceleration: 18 + 16 =
Top speed: 7 x 8 =
Turbo power: 45 - 34 =
Total:

Acceleration: 70 - 60 =
Top speed: 15 + 26 =
Turbo power: 9 x 6 =
Total:

Acceleration: 12 x 3 =
Top speed: 84 - 54 =
Turbo power: 32 + 14 =
Total:

Acceleration: 99 - 81 =
Top speed: 11 x 4 =
Turbo power: 21 + 23 =
Total:

Find and circle 11 footprints...
...3 aliens...
...a biting plant...
...and a camera.

Join these even-numbered dots in number order, starting with the smallest, to see how Patrick travels around on the planet's surface.

Number these pictures in historical order by writing 1, 2, 3 and 4 in the white stars, starting with the oldest.

52

The answers to the calculations on the smaller screen are hidden in the grid below. Can you find and circle them? They may be written across or down, but not diagonally, backwards or up.

8	2	3	7	2	6	0	2
3	1	8	0	1	0	7	5
4	8	3	5	9	8	3	0
2	9	6	0	1	7	5	8
7	0	3	4	0	6	1	9
5	3	8	0	6	2	8	3
0	9	0	3	0	1	6	0

11 + 12

30 − 13

5 x 5

60 − 21

19 + 9

6 x 8

75 − 24

18 + 18

It is 9:30am. Can Robbie spend 10 minutes looking at each exhibit with a yellow star symbol, and still make it to the show in the planetarium?

Which silhouette matches this picture?

A

B

C

Are there enough pieces of space junk for each pilot to collect five?

Help mission control find the code, ready for countdown. Use the totals for each row and column to find out which 3 numbers the symbols stand for, and write the answers below.

A glitch in the software has scrambled 12 of the words in this email. Can you find them and work out what they should say?

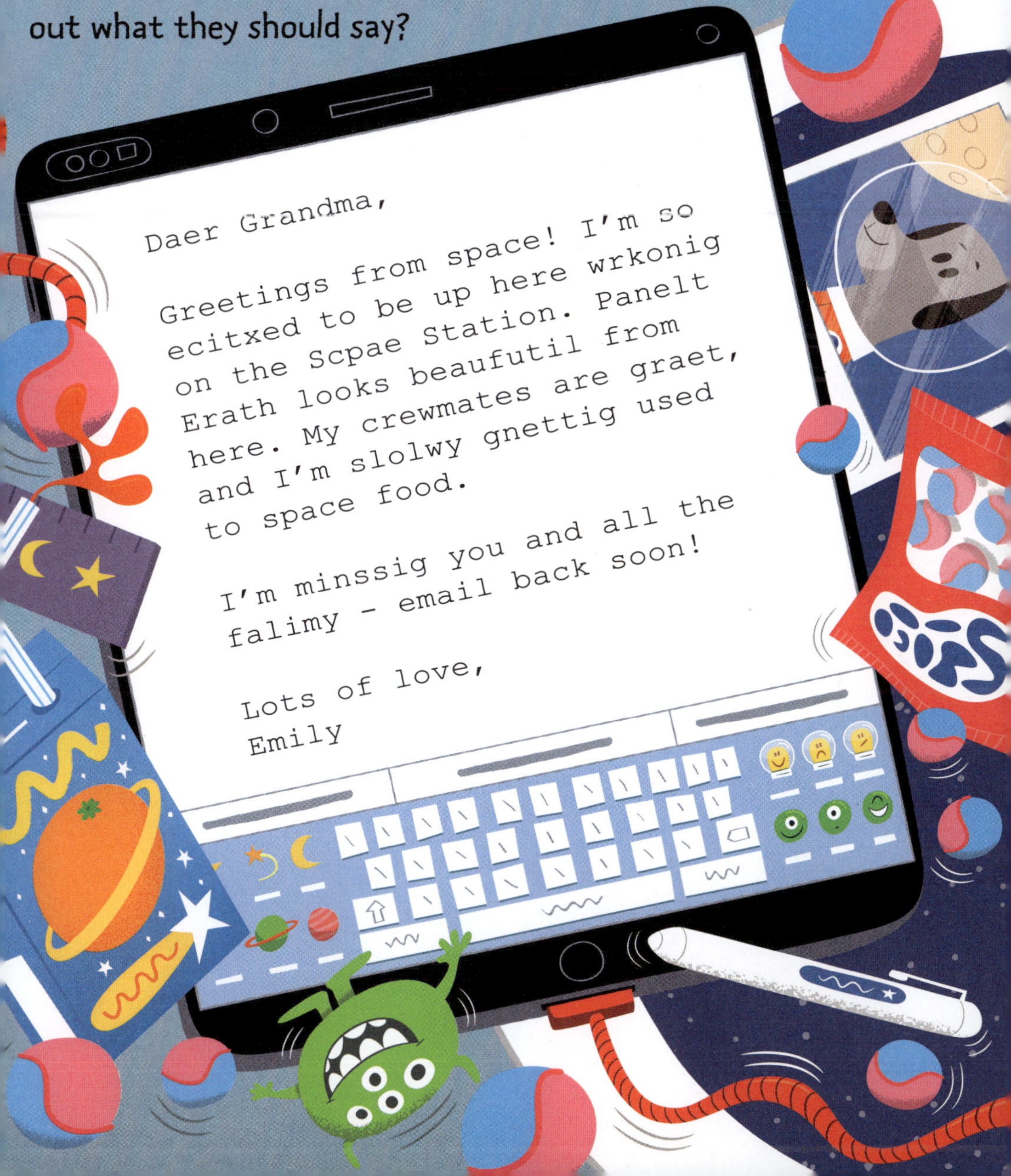

Daer Grandma,

Greetings from space! I'm so ecitxed to be up here wrkonig on the Scpae Station. Panelt Erath looks beaufutil from here. My crewmates are graet, and I'm slolwy gnettig used to space food.

I'm minssig you and all the falimy - email back soon!

Lots of love,
Emily

These astronauts are experimenting with growing plants in space. Draw the correct number of seedlings in each pod.

- Pod B has twice as many seedlings as Pod C
- Pod D has one less than Pod B
- Pod A has two more than Pod D

Fill in the shapes that have orange spots to see the hidden picture.

This grid is made up of 6 blocks, each with 6 squares. Fill in the blank squares so that each block, row and column contains all the numbers 1 to 6.

	3	1			6
6		5			
3				2	5
2		6	4		
5	4				2
			5	3	

Which constellation is Doug looking at? The number of stars he can see is odd, and can be divided by 3.

Spot 5 differences between the pictures below.

Circle the words that can't be made with letters from the word ASTEROID. Each letter can be used only once.

The astronauts are doing a timed sample collection test as part of their rover training. Add up Mia's times. Has she passed?

66

On each of the rows below, find the sequence and then draw the correct design in the final screen.

Link the moons below to spell three space words. Each word has one letter in each orbit, and starts in the orbit closest to the planet Zap, moving outwards.

Katarina needs to fix the two identical satellites.
Can you find them?

Can you find out where each crate of space food should be delivered? Do the calculations, then draw a line from each pod to its matching crate.

Circle the 4 pieces at the bottom of the page that complete the picture.

If all the spacecraft you can see park at the Park & Zoom for two days, how many zorps will Plonzod the parking bot collect altogether?

Can you circle these 5 parts of the picture?

Can you help direct the spaceship back to the crew's home planet, moving from square to square in the order shown? It can move across, up and down, but not diagonally.

Can you unscramble the labels for the space suit and write them on the dotted lines below?

Can you help Henry find his friend Pippa? She has dark hair with a bow, and she's holding a guidebook.

Shade in the squares containing odd numbers to see the hidden picture.

2	20	50	40	62	18	64	46	22	34	60	62	42	36	64	50	44	26	56	16	90	22	60	10	26
12	32	34	21	60	12	52	54	86	43	28	56	28	66	4	96	60	4	34	22	58	6	30	46	14
36	86	52	36	13	34	20	82	71	46	50	22	16	14	62	12	34	40	24	10	40	54	34	2	58
8	54	12	53	51	75	97	81	23	15	38	14	6	50	34	17	18	96	8	46	96	23	54	34	42
64	72	9	31	8	43	57	79	34	91	35	20	18	6	92	34	65	34	70	34	99	94	62	30	48
54	53	75	97	19	37	51	23	35	65	87	91	26	34	24	81	53	87	79	33	27	61	92	36	40
34	5	12	11	27	43	44	65	87	65	54	33	84	30	35	67	22	19	35	49	18	73	59	12	92
26	73	58	7	54	34	26	56	40	9	80	27	78	41	39	57	73	61	93	85	9	15	63	25	58
54	62	46	55	20	30	6	32	68	61	32	40	26	37	34	17	21	9	82	51	43	27	48	91	20
36	40	82	90	33	24	96	58	47	92	10	36	18	29	52	25	60	68	40	46	28	35	50	7	38
34	30	44	26	66	42	78	22	34	58	24	42	36	60	22	67	16	34	18	36	84	91	44	40	16
12	22	40	86	28	20	14	70	18	16	90	34	20	52	28	34	21	32	62	78	27	16	12	58	52
66	30	52	6	34	96	28	30	28	34	2	48	42	34	66	12	66	48	92	44	50	22	28	34	10
22	10	42	36	18	20	29	48	76	60	32	64	2	12	34	14	54	18	26	38	46	32	60	16	50
2	62	44	78	22	76	67	66	18	10	82	26	54	64	90	34	10	58	60	4	20	92	2	14	44
34	40	4	16	8	98	34	78	56	34	12	30	66	56	18	34	80	24	34	90	56	98	70	52	60
14	30	36	32	90	10	56	18	62	6	60	20	42	4	32	62	58	40	48	38	74	8	34	64	6
44	66	98	22	42	60	43	40	46	34	50	34	22	54	26	34	16	34	43	64	14	56	24	52	48
48	2	60	28	52	99	35	29	56	94	8	98	34	14	12	50	46	35	71	95	66	34	28	36	50
8	58	32	12	31	65	41	39	11	16	60	38	2	34	90	28	73	51	79	45	87	16	6	88	24

Fill in the grid so that all four symbols appear in every row and column.

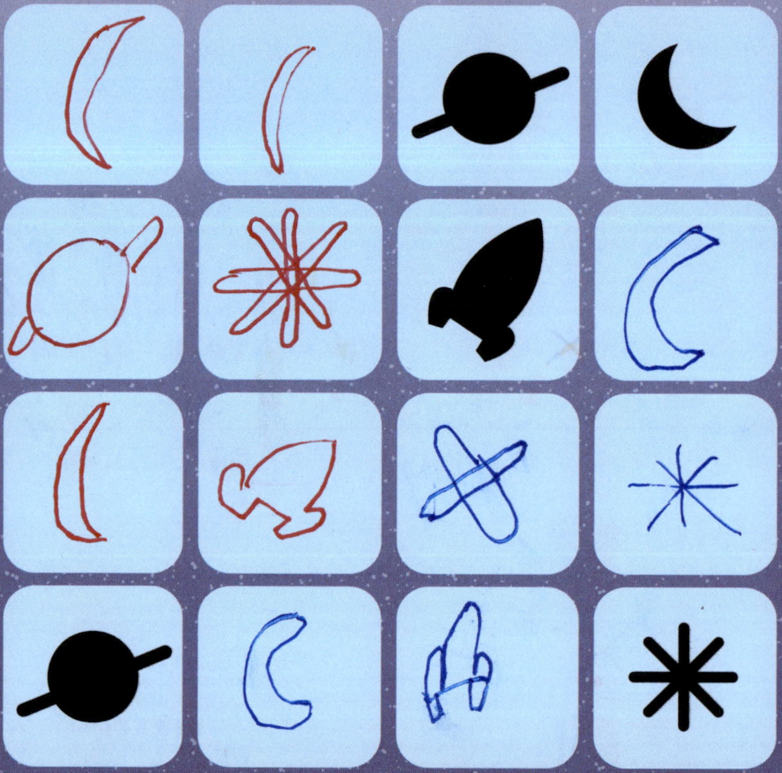

Join these odd-numbered dots in number order, starting with the smallest, to see how Froglod is flying around the galaxy.

Fill in the blank screens so that the satellites show the numbers 1–9, using each number only once. The numbers on each side of the triangle must add up to 20.

Write a word on each section of the launch tower that can be made by changing just one letter of the word before it. There is a clue for each word to help you.

Can you find and circle the 9 blue bolts that Ali the astronaut needs to repair the space station?

Circle the 3 pieces at the bottom of the page that complete the picture.

Look at the clocks below and circle the spaceship that completed the race in the fastest time.

The fastest ever flight time on the Planet Plurg Ring Racetrack is 56 seconds. Add up Alienna's times on the signs. Has she beaten the record? Circle yes or no.

Find and circle 2 pairs of glasses...

...an alarm clock...

...3 apples...

...a ball...

...and a mouse.

Ziggy and Zog are organizing deliveries to planet Poptik's moons, and they need to make sure that each item arrives at the correct time. Read the information on the screen, then write the name of each moon under the correct clock.

Spot 5 differences between the pictures below.

88

Which of the flying saucers at the bottom of the page comes next in the sequence?

Can you find a path through the panel, passing through the letters of the word ROCKET in the correct order?

Write all the numbers 1 to 9 in the grid, so the 4 squares around each circle add up to the circle's total, and the red, green and blue areas add up to the totals shown at the bottom. Some have been filled in for you.

Draw the other half of this alien, using the grid to help you.

Plorp is packing for his intergalactic travels. Spend one minute looking at the things that he's put in his suitcase so far, then turn over and circle the three new items he's added.

Look at the other side of the page to find out how to do this puzzle.

Can you complete the words by joining up pairs of rocks?

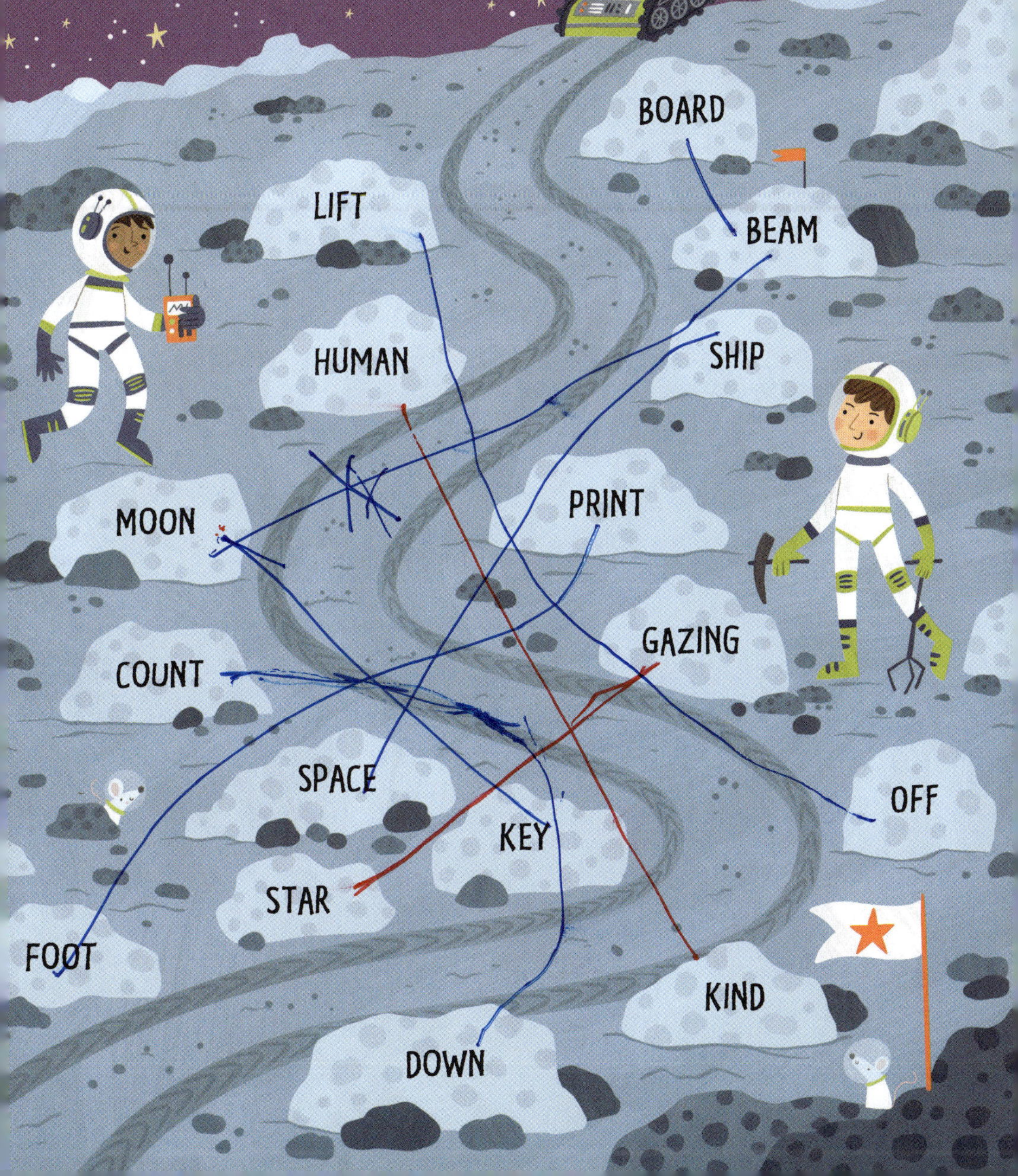

The scoreboard at the Galactic Games shows how many points the teams win for each event. Can you complete the scores by filling in the missing numbers?

>>> GALACTIC GAMES RESULTS >>>

	Long jump	Jet pack race	Space golf	TOTAL
Cosmic Ray's Racers	18	20	23	
Astro Athletic		22		**60**
Team Moonbeam	12		25	**58**
TOTAL	**45**			

Help the spaceship find a path along the white lines back to Earth. It can pass stars, but not the other obstacles.

Can you spot the rover that is different from all the others?

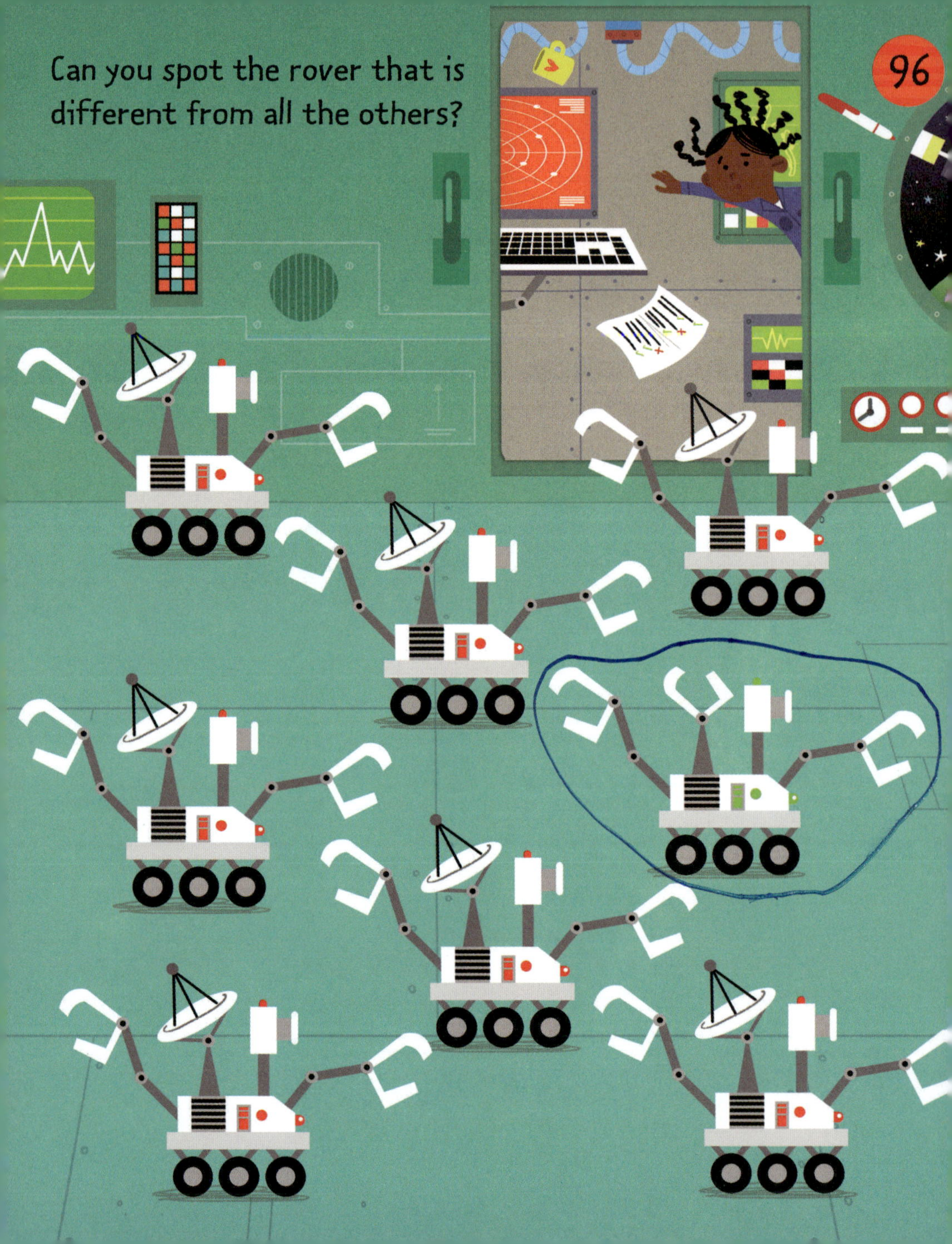

Each time a student gave a correct answer in astronomy class, they earned a star credit.

- George received seven credits
- Megan earned three more credits than Anita
- Anita was given two more credits than George
- Poppy received half as many credits as Megan

Write each student's score on the Star Credits chart.

Fill in the blank squares so that each block, row and column contains all six letters of the word PLANET.

N	T				P
		T	P		L
	L	E	N		A
	P	L	E		N
A		P	T		
L					T

Which silhouette matches this picture?

A

B

C

Amar needs to come back in through the airlock. Help Anya find the door release code by filling in the shapes containing green dots. Write the code on the dotted lines.

When their timers reach zero, the astronauts need to return to the space station. Who will be the last one to go back?

Can you find all the animals that have been to space in the grid below?

E	N	O	T	S	F	L	V	E	R
S	E	F	R	U	I	T	F	L	Y
T	H	Z	G	L	S	A	O	R	M
O	G	U	N	W	H	W	D	A	Y
R	L	O	X	A	T	S	R	B	E
T	O	H	D	A	P	G	E	B	W
O	W	Y	C	I	O	M	D	I	O
I	M	O	N	K	E	Y	I	T	P
S	I	P	N	Y	H	O	P	H	A
E	M	E	T	M	O	U	S	E	C

TORTOISE
MONKEY

CHIMPANZEE
FRUIT FLY

DOG
CAT

FISH
MOUSE

RABBIT
SPIDER

Yuri needs to charge his laptop. Can you help him find a charger that's already plugged into a power terminal?

104

This grid is made up of 9 blocks, each with 9 squares. Fill in the blank squares so that each block, row and column contains all the numbers 1 to 9.

2		1		9	8			
	6	3		5	1	9		7
4	5		7				8	
	9	6			3		4	5
	8		5	1		6		
		7	2		9	3		
7	2			3		4		6
		4		8			5	1
9			6		7			2

Can you circle these 5 parts of the picture?

Solve the clues in the grid, writing the answers in the direction of the arrows, with one letter in each box. The first one has been done for you.

May appear in the sky when it rains			Opposite of new		
M	A	R	B	L	E
Small, round, glass toy			Tiny grains seen at the beach		A jumping animal found near ponds
Hard-working insects		There isn't any of this in space			
It goes around the Earth		A furry, barking pet			

Astronaut Andy is repairing the satellite.
Circle the one piece he won't need to use.

Can you find 8 space words in the spiral?

Which spaceship is going to get a parking ticket? It has a red body, a circular window and a tailfin at the back.

Can you help mission control figure out the sequence and fill in the missing numbers ready for take-off?

			7		11
13			19		23
	27			33	
37					47
	51		55		59
61		65		69	

Which UFO is on the spaceship's radar screen?
Circle the one that matches the silhouette.

Use the code below to find out what the little aliens are learning at school today.

Five passengers can ride in the space elevator pod at once. How many trips will be needed to transport everyone in the picture up to the Space Hotel?

Follow the trails and write the correct charger number next to each spaceship.

Harry has a flight simulator test tomorrow morning, but there are tasks he must complete before the test. Can you help him decide what time to get up?

Harry needs to set his alarm clock for ....

Draw a line between each bootprint and the moon boot that made it.

Gribble and Grooble are racing back to their home planet. Add up the times on the sensors to see who will arrive first, and write the winner's name on the sign.

Find a way for Ellie to pick up all the radio transmitters on the ground and return to the landing pod, without taking the same route twice.

Which square at the bottom is not part of the picture?

Can you help the aliens find a way through the nebula back to the mothership?

Can you find these spacecraft names in the grid?

P	N	O	T	S	O	Y	U	Z	R
I	E	A	F	K	H	N	P	C	V
O	G	N	G	L	N	S	O	L	O
N	I	U	D	W	L	U	D	H	Y
E	O	L	X	E	A	G	L	E	A
E	T	O	N	P	A	Z	H	T	G
R	T	Y	O	I	O	V	S	A	E
A	O	L	U	A	M	J	O	P	R
Y	L	V	I	K	I	N	G	U	A
O	M	A	R	I	N	E	R	H	R

APOLLO
ENDEAVOUR
GIOTTO
MARINER
EAGLE
SOYUZ
VOYAGER
PIONEER
VIKING
LUNA

Are there more green spaceships or purple spaceships?

Answer: ......purple......

Can you help the astronauts put the food packets in the correct places by writing the names on the signs?

- The apples go between the mushrooms and bananas
- The bananas go underneath the oranges
- The beans go next to the carrots

Match up the words with opposite meanings.
Which flag isn't part of a pair?

Astronaut Alfie needs to get some samples to the lab, but whichever path he takes, there are obstacles that add time to his journey. Draw along the quickest route.

All the server lights must be green before the rocket can launch. Can you find the quickest way for Bryony to check all the red lights and then report to Bob, without crossing her own path or running into anyone else?

Can you find the route through the galaxy by moving from square to square in the sequence shown at the bottom? You can't move diagonally, or go through any box more than once.

Complete these space jokes by matching the questions with their punchlines.

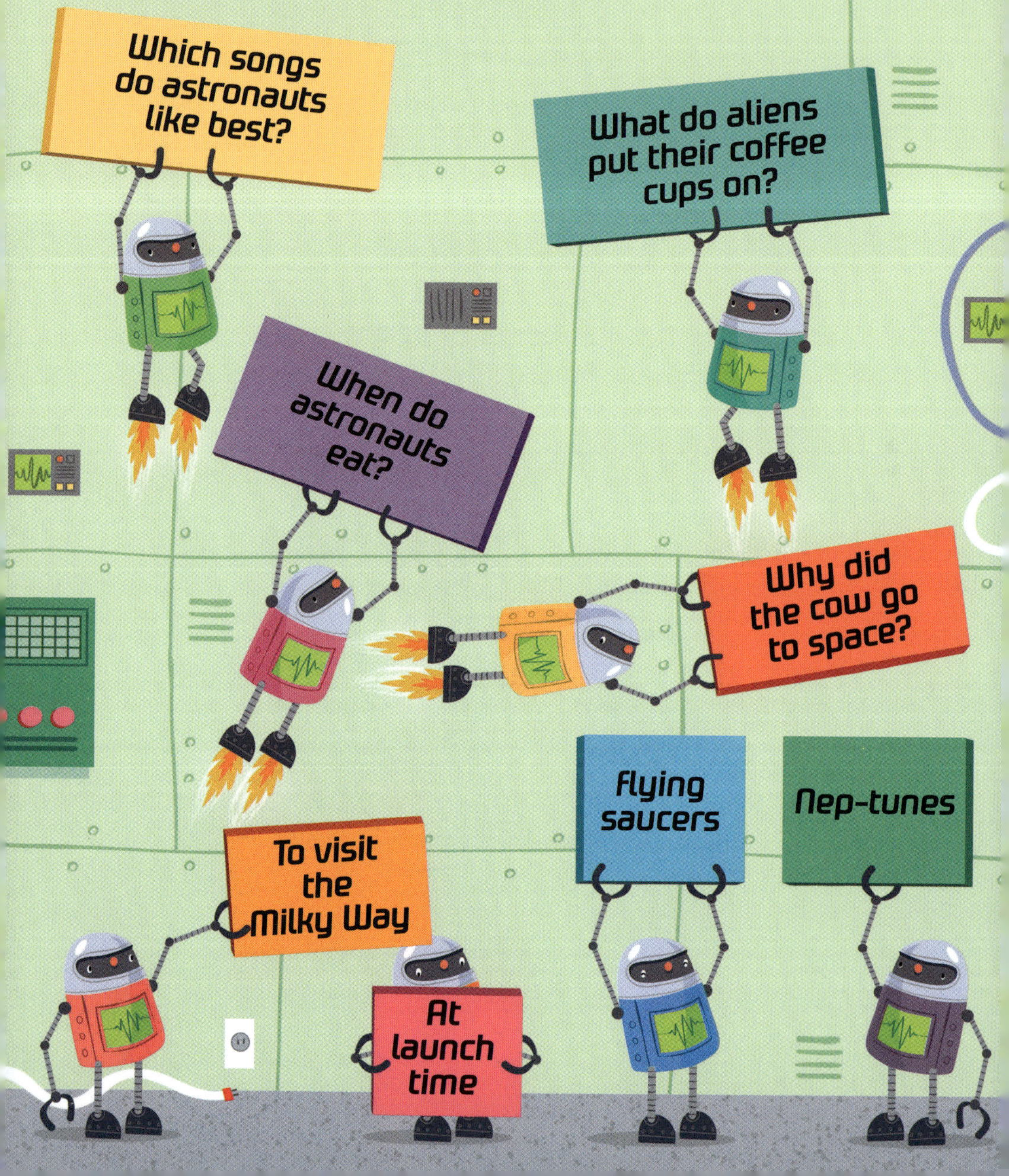

Can you find these constellation names in the grid?

R	N	O	T	S	G	L	P	E	A
S	F	P	O	R	I	O	N	I	U
U	H	E	G	C	N	A	E	L	R
R	S	G	I	A	A	P	D	H	S
U	Z	A	X	R	O	S	A	O	A
A	T	S	N	I	C	R	U	X	M
T	W	U	S	N	O	N	S	L	A
N	H	S	V	A	M	I	Y	P	J
E	A	P	D	Y	D	R	A	C	O
C	M	O	E	L	A	S	T	H	R

LEO
CRUX
DRACO

PEGASUS
CENTAURUS
CASSIOPEIA
URSA MAJOR

LYRA
ORION
CARINA

Help Captain Colin beam the astronauts back aboard the ship by writing their names in alphabetical order in the transporter.

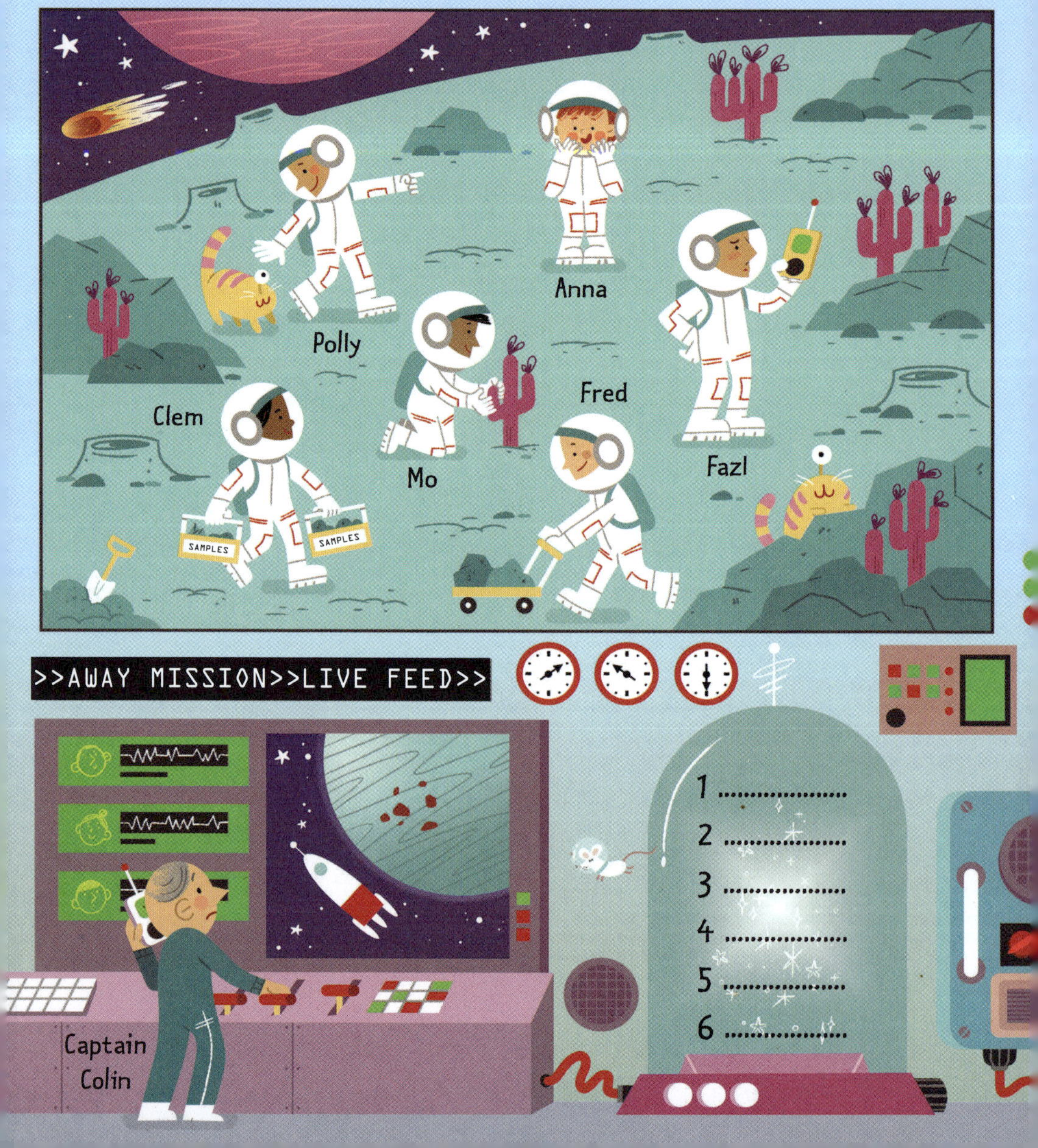

Spot 3 differences between the pictures below.

Which of these lunar landing pods is the odd one out?

At the Space Mall, Milo spends exactly 50 credits on 3 different items. Which ones does he buy?

Find these two groups of planets in the picture below.

Help Sammy the Salvage Bot collect all the green parts of the satellite and take them back to its workshop. It can't go along the same path twice.

Solve the clues to fill in the blank spaces below.

ACROSS

3. Name for our galaxy (5, 3)
4. Giant ball of blazing gas in space (4)
7. Space explorer (9)
9. All the galaxies together make up the __________ (8)
10. Our local 4 across is named the ___ (3)
11. Move around a star or planet (5)

DOWN

1. Very large round object that goes around a star (6)
2. The Red Planet (4)
5. Big lump of rock, ice and metal in space (8)
6. Large round object that goes around a planet (4)
8. The Ringed Planet (6)

Are there enough craters for three aliens to live in each one?

Answers

1. Yes

2.

3.

4.

5.

6.

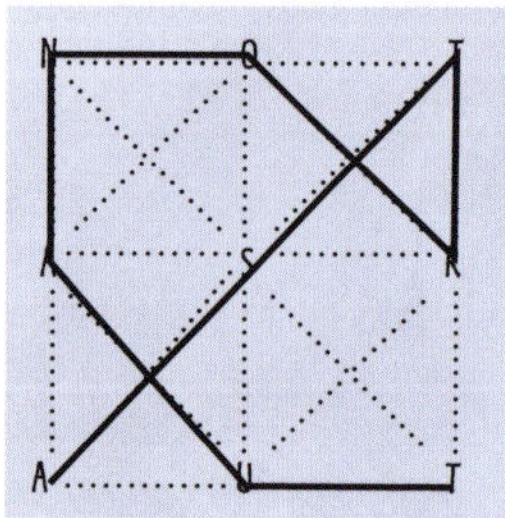

Astronaut

7. 16 squares

8.

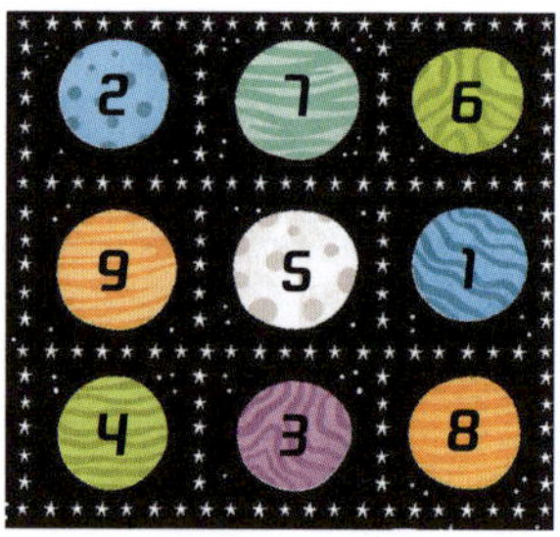

9.

10.

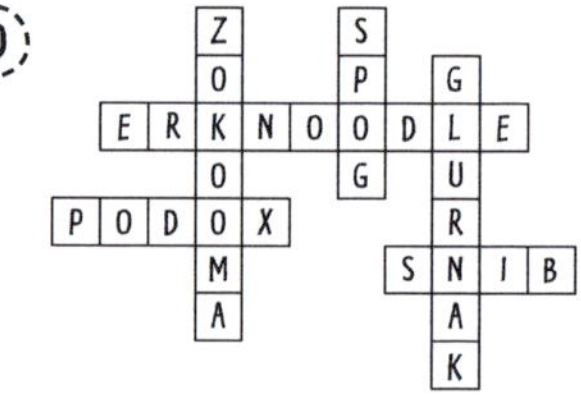

11.

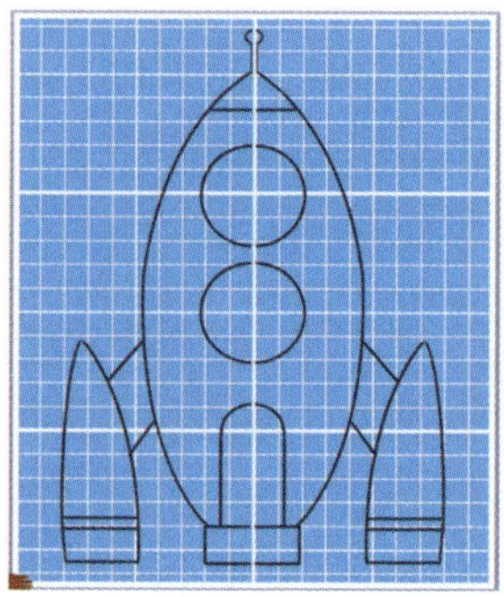

Answers

12 

13 

14 

15 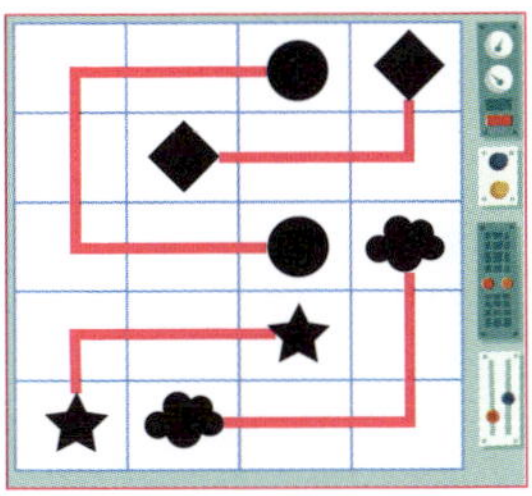

16 

17 ROCKET, EXPLORE, ORBIT, LAUNCH, PLANET, MISSION, GALAXY, SHUTTLE

18 

19 

20 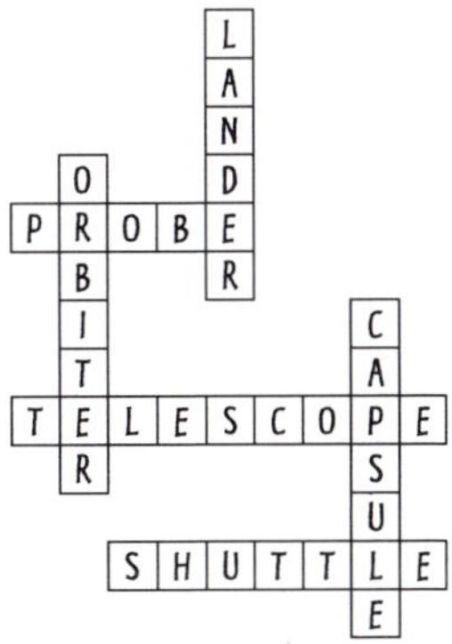

21 1st: Zooble
2nd: Frimp
3rd: Urk
4th: Splog
5th: Zid

Answers

(22)

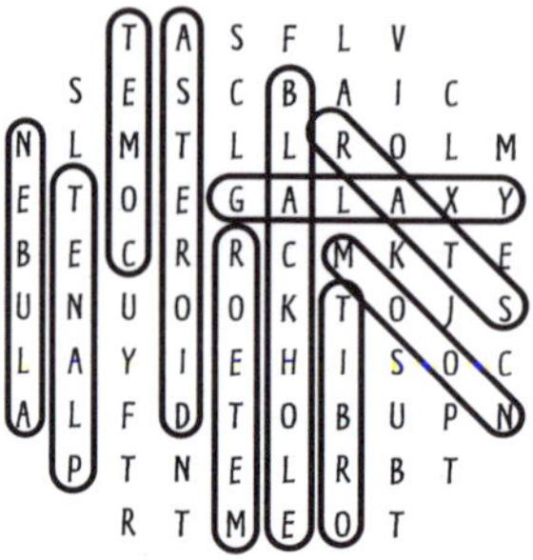

(23) 1 hour 30 = 90 mins

= 1 orbit

3 hours = 180 mins

= 2 orbits

45 mins

= 1/2 an orbit

(24)

(25)

TOOL
TOOT
BOOT
BOLT
BELT

(26)

(27) Nanobot 1

(28) WELCOME TO OUR PLANET

(29)

(30)

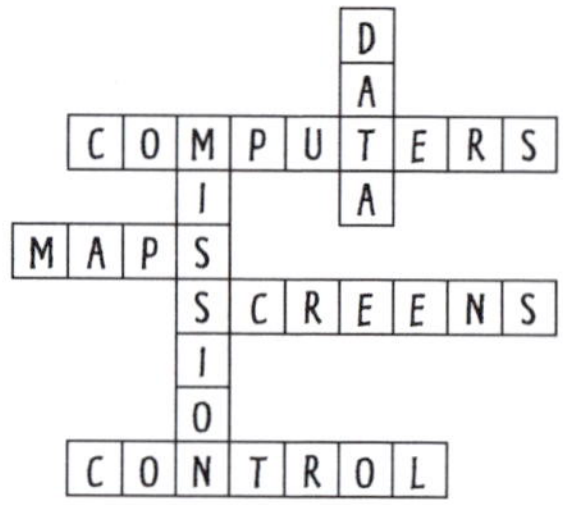

(31)

(32) Yes

Answers

33 More with 3 eyes
(9 aliens with 3 eyes,
5 aliens with 4 eyes)

34 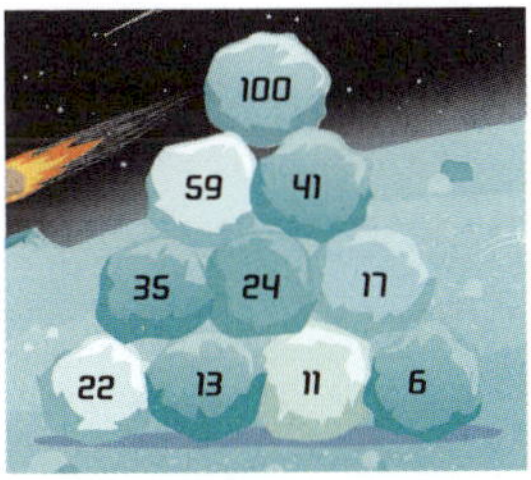

35 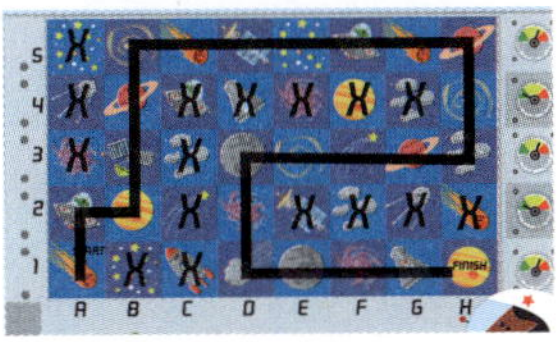

36 

37 

38 

39 

40 

41 

42 Bella: 6
Bill: 12

43

R	A	S	T
S	T	A	R
A	R	T	S
T	S	R	A

Answers

44

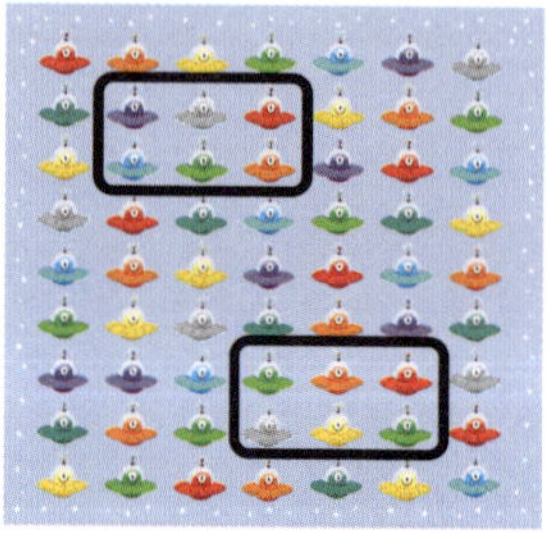

47

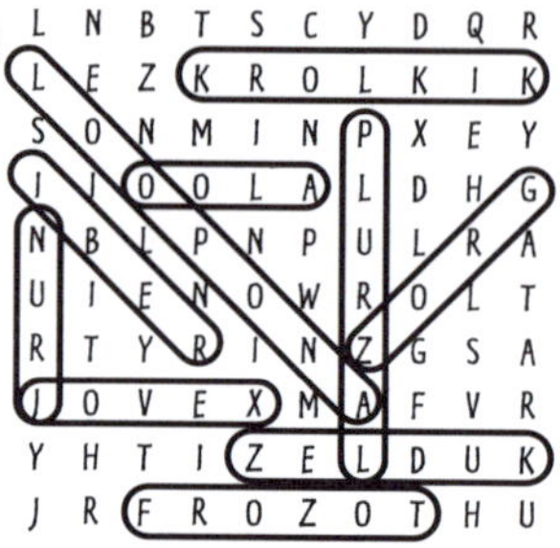

51

45

48 Annabel is exploring Venus.

49

52

1. The Romans: 8th century BC - 5th century AD
2. Galileo Galilei: 16th-17th century AD
3. Albert Einstein: 20th century AD
4. 21st century AD

46

4	6	3	2	1	5
2	1	5	3	6	4
6	5	1	4	3	2
3	4	2	6	5	1
5	2	6	1	4	3
1	3	4	5	2	6

50

Answers

53 

11 + 12 = 23
30 - 13 = 17
5 x 5 = 25
60 - 21 = 39
19 + 9 = 28
6 x 8 = 48
75 - 24 = 51
18 + 18 = 36

54 Yes. There are 5 exhibits with yellow stars, so he will spend 50 minutes in the gallery, finishing at 10:20am.

55 B

56 Yes. There are 21 pieces of space junk and 4 pilots.

57 

58 **Dear** Grandma,

Greetings from space! I'm so **excited** to be up here **working** on the **Space** Station. **Planet Earth** looks **beautiful** from here. My crewmates are **great**, and I'm **slowly getting** used to space food.

I'm **missing** you and all the **family** - email back soon!

Lots of love,
Emily

59 

60 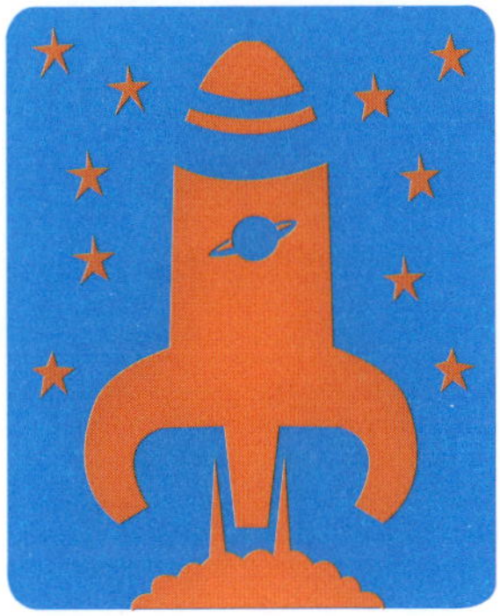

61

4	3	1	2	5	6
6	2	5	3	4	1
3	1	4	6	2	5
2	5	6	4	1	3
5	4	3	1	6	2
1	6	2	5	3	4

Answers

62 

Leo

63 

64 

65 Mia took
34 seconds,
so she passed.

66 

67 STAR, MOON, RING

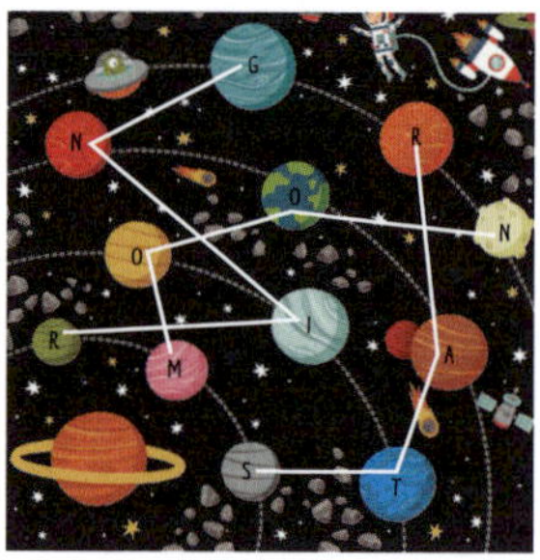

68 

69 

70 

71 24 zorps
(4 x 3 = 12
12 x 2 = 24)

Answers

72

73

74

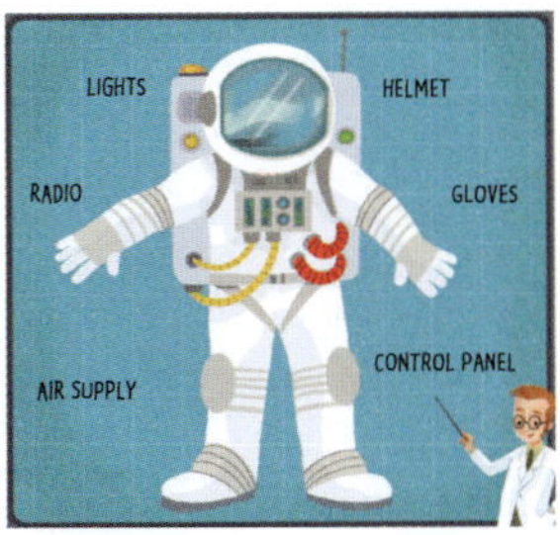

75

76

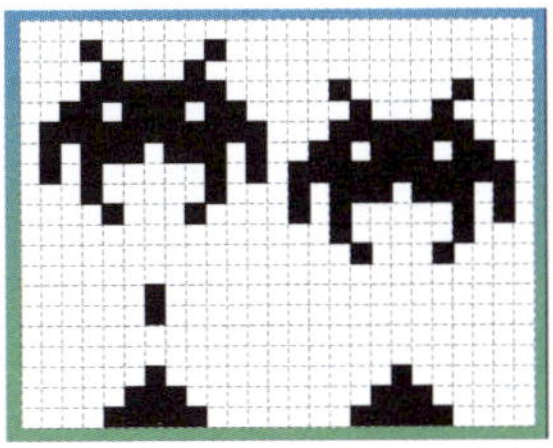

77

78

79

80

MOON
SOON
SOOT
SHOT
SHOP
SHIP

Answers

81

82

83

Purple: 28 minutes
Blue: 38 minutes
Green: 26 minutes
Red: 29 minutes

84 No: Alienna's time was 60 seconds.

85

86

87

88

(Sequence: orange, blue, purple, green)

89

90

91

Answers

2

95

98

N	T	A	L	E	P
E	A	T	P	N	L
P	L	E	N	T	A
T	P	L	E	A	N
A	N	P	T	L	E
L	E	N	A	P	T

99 C

3 COUNT - DOWN
MOON - BEAM
KEY - BOARD
LIFT - OFF
SPACE - SHIP
HUMAN - KIND
STAR - GAZING
FOOT - PRINT

96

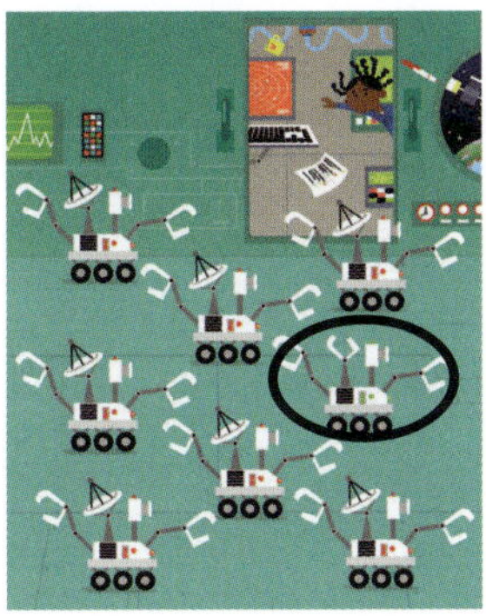

100 Code: 8741

101

97 Anita: 9
Megan: 12
Poppy: 6
George: 7

4

	Long jump	Jet pack race	Space golf	TOTAL
Cosmic Ray's Racers	18	20	23	**61**
Astro Athletic	15	22	23	**60**
Team Moonbeam	12	21	25	**58**
TOTAL	**45**	**63**	**71**	**179**

Answers

102

E	N	O	T	S	F	L	V	E	R
S	E	F	R	U	I	T	F	L	Y
T	H	Z	G	L	S	A	O	R	M
O	G	U	N	W	H	W	D	A	Y
R	L	O	X	A	T	S	R	B	E
T	O	H	D	A	P	G	E	B	W
O	W	Y	C	I	O	M	D	I	O
I	M	O	N	K	E	Y	I	T	P
S	I	P	N	Y	H	O	P	H	A
E	M	E	T	M	O	U	S	E	C

105

108 UNIVERSE, STAR, PLANET, SATELLITE, ORBIT, SHUTTLE, MOON, COMET

103 E

106

May appear in the sky when it rains	R		Opposite of new	O	
M	A	R	B	L	E
Small, round, glass toy	I		Tiny grains seen at the beach	D	A jumping animal found near ponds
A	N	T	S		F
Hard-working insects	B	There isn't any of this in space	A	I	R
M	O	O	N		O
It goes around the Earth	W	A furry, barking pet	D	O	G

109

104

2	7	1	3	9	8	5	6	4
8	6	3	4	5	1	9	2	7
4	5	9	7	2	6	1	8	3
1	9	6	8	7	3	2	4	5
3	8	2	5	1	4	6	7	9
5	4	7	2	6	9	3	1	8
7	2	8	1	3	5	4	9	6
6	3	4	9	8	2	7	5	1
9	1	5	6	4	7	8	3	2

107

110

1	3	5	7	9	11
13	15	17	19	21	23
25	27	29	31	33	35
37	39	41	43	45	47
49	51	53	55	57	59
61	63	65	67	69	71

Answers

111 

116 

120 

112 Humans live on planet Earth.

117 Gribble: 24 seconds
Grooble: 26 seconds
Gribble wins.

121 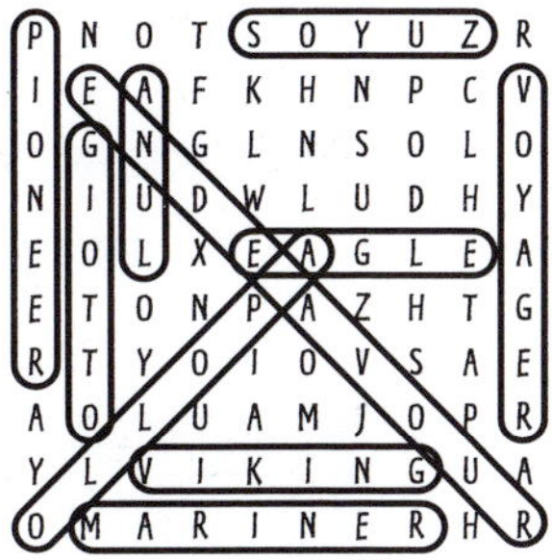

113 3 trips

114 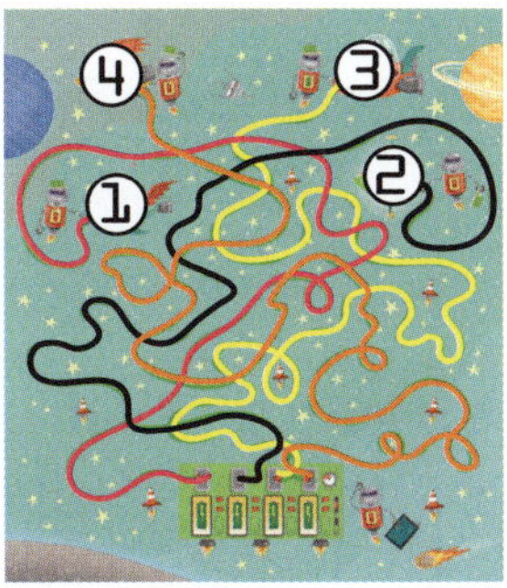

118 

122 More purple spaceships (6 green, 7 purple)

123 

115 Harry needs to set his alarm clock for 7:45am.

119 

Answers

124 AWAKE – ASLEEP
BEFORE – AFTER
LOUD – QUIET
DAWN – DUSK
EARLY – LATE
PUSH – PULL
UP – DOWN
EAST isn't part of a pair.

125 

126 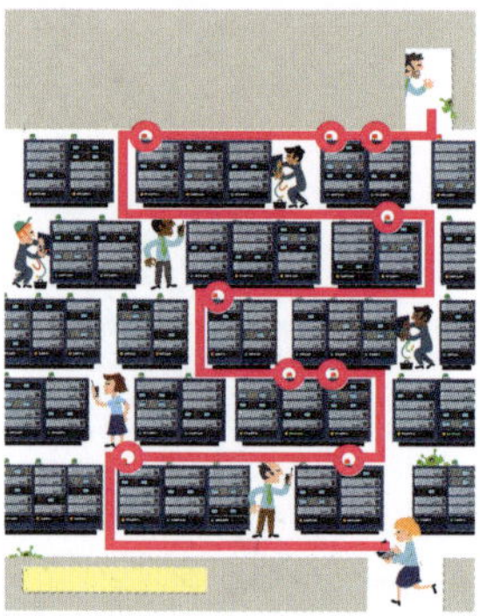

127 

128 Which songs do astronauts like best?
Nep-tunes
What do aliens put their coffee cups on?
Flying saucers
When do astronauts eat?
At launch time
Why did the cow go to space?
To visit the Milky Way

129 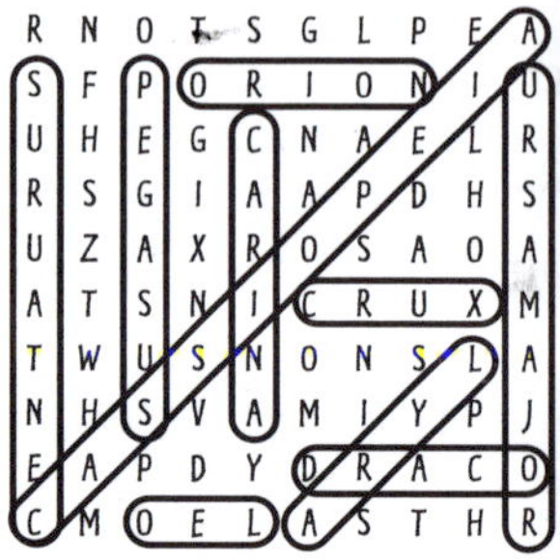

130 1. Anna 2. Clem
3. Fazl 4. Fred
5. Mo 6. Polly

131 

132